USBORNE
FIRST BOOK OF THE
PIANO

Eileen O'Brien and John C. Miles

Designed by Jan McCafferty
Illustrated by Simone Abel
Edited by Caroline Hooper

Original music and arrangements by
Eileen O'Brien and Barrie Carson Turner

Series editor: Jane Chisholm

About this book

This book is about learning to play the piano. It explains how the piano works, and shows you how to read music and play tunes.

You can find out how music is written down on pages 8 and 9.

Playing tunes

You can learn to play different sounds, called notes, on your piano. As soon as you have learned the first few notes, there are tunes for you to play.

At first, the tunes are fairly easy, but they get harder as you go through the book.

Each time you learn something new, there is a tune to help you practise it.

There are lots of playing tips and advice on practising.

You will probably have heard some of the tunes before.

Others have been specially written for this book.

Music words and symbols

As well as learning notes, you can also learn about music words and symbols.

As you go through the book, you can find out what symbols like these mean.

Piano facts

Throughout the book, there are amazing facts about pianos. You can find out when the first piano was made, and how big the world's biggest piano was.

There are also lots of puzzles to help you learn.

You will find answers to all of the puzzles at the end of the book.

Your piano

Before you start playing, you can find out about the piano and how it works on these pages.

How a piano works

Ask someone to open the top lid of your piano. Stand on a chair and look inside. You will see lots of strings.

Each key is attached to a hammer inside the piano. When you press a key, the hammer hits a string. This makes the sound.

Strings

Hammers

This is what happens inside a piano when you press a key.

This is a stand to hold the music up.

This section is called the keyboard.

These are called keys.

These are foot pedals.

Pressing the pedals changes the sound the piano makes.

You don't need to use the pedals for the tunes in this book.

Getting comfortable

You can usually raise or lower your piano stool until it is the correct height for you. If you don't have a piano stool, you could try chairs of different heights, or use a cushion.

Your stool, or chair, is the right height...

...when your elbows are in line with the keys.

Playing tip

Keep your wrist, elbow, and the tips of your fingers in a straight line.

Your fingers should be slightly curved.

You can practise this by laying your arm and hand along a flat surface.

Sitting at your piano

Try to relax before you start to play, and make sure you are sitting comfortably on your stool or chair. Put this book on the music stand.

Try to keep your back straight.

Don't hunch your shoulders.

You must be able to reach the keys easily without stretching.

Sit directly in front of the pedals.

Hold your elbows slightly away from the sides of your body.

Musical notes

Music is made up from lots of sounds called notes. You can play notes on your piano by pressing the keys. Each key plays a different note.

Finding notes

The black and white keys on your piano are arranged in a regular pattern. This pattern is repeated all along the keyboard of the piano. You can use this pattern to work out the names of the notes.

Finding middle C

One of the most important notes on the piano is called middle C. The key that plays middle C is just to the left of two black keys, nearest the middle of the piano.

High and low notes

There is a word for how high or low a note sounds. This is called its pitch. The higher a note sounds, the higher its pitch. The lower a note sounds, the lower its pitch.

Note game

Try to find and play the groups of four notes in this box. Read the lines down or across.

Writing music down

Music is written on a set of five lines called a staff. Each note has its own place on the staff. Some go on the lines, and others go in the spaces between the lines.

Piano music

The word for more than one staff is staves. Most piano music is written on two staves, one for each hand. At the beginning of each staff, there is a special sign called a clef.

Your first note

On page 7, you found out how to play middle C. Here you can find out how this note is written down.

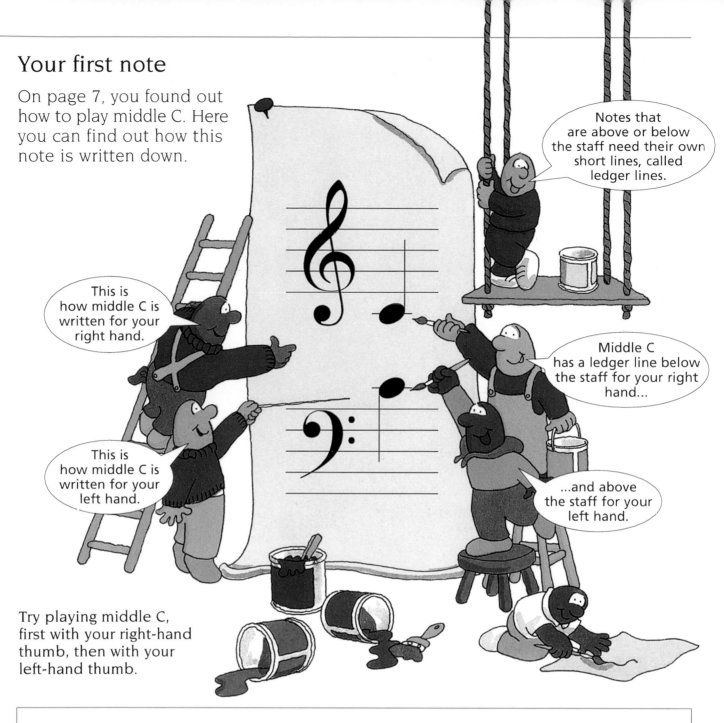

Try playing middle C, first with your right-hand thumb, then with your left-hand thumb.

Piano fact

The first piano was made around 1710 by an Italian called Bartolomeo Cristofori. The real name for a piano is *pianoforte*. In Italian, *piano* means "quiet", and *forte* means "loud". You can play both quietly and loudly on a piano.

Counting

Music is made up of notes of different lengths. You measure the lengths by counting. The pattern of counts in a tune is called its rhythm.

A rhythm is made up of a series of counts, or beats.

There are rhythms all around you.

The ticking of a clock and the beating of a drum are both rhythms.

Clapping a rhythm

Say the words below and clap as you say them. Try to make each clap last the same length of time.

Sold - iers march - ing, left, right, left, right
clap clap clap clap clap clap clap clap

You are clapping the simplest rhythm...

...where all the beats are the same length.

Counting a rhythm

When you are playing, you can't clap at the same time. Instead you have to count to keep the rhythm steady.

A one-count note

In music, different note shapes tell you how many beats to count for each note A note that lasts for one beat is called a crotchet.

The rhythm you clapped on page 10 looks like this. There is one crotchet for each clap.

Writing rhythms down

When music is written down on a staff, the counts are divided into groups. These groups are called bars.

How long is each bar?

There are numbers at the beginning of a tune to tell you how many counts there are in each bar. These numbers are called the time signature.

Your first tunes

Here are two tunes for you to play. They are both in four-four time. Look at the clefs to see which hands to use.

Longer notes

A note that lasts for two beats is called a minim. It looks like a white crotchet.

A note that lasts for four beats is called a semibreve. It looks like a minim without a stem.

Clapping a rhythm

Try clapping this rhythm. The numbers under the rhythm will help you.

C *tune*

Here is a tune for you to play. It uses all the different types of notes you have learned so far.

Using different fingers

In piano music, you will often see a number next to a note. This tells you which finger to use to play that note. Here you can see which number goes with each finger.

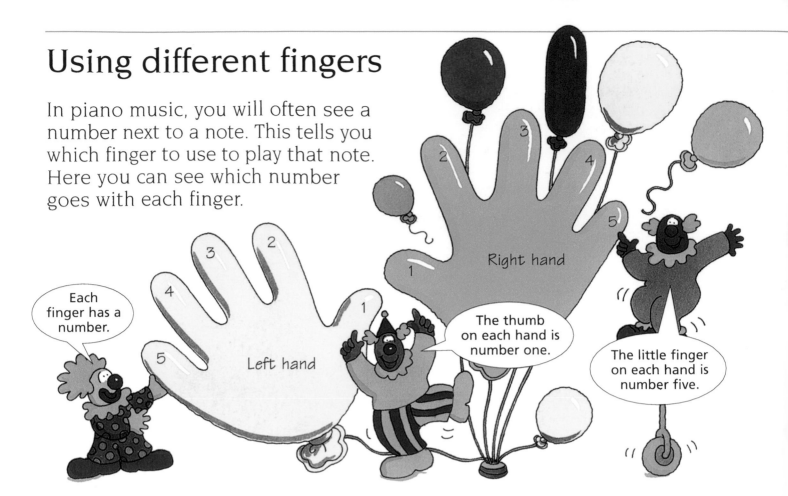

Each finger has a number.

Left hand

Right hand

The thumb on each hand is number one.

The little finger on each hand is number five.

Playing smoothly

Here you can find out how to play the notes in a tune more smoothly.

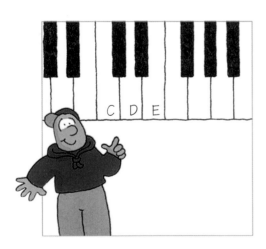

C D E

Press the keys shown above, starting with C. Use your first finger only. You have to take your finger off each note before playing the next one.

Press these keys again, one after the other. This time, use your right thumb for C, your first finger for D, and your middle finger for E.

Start to press the next key down as you are lifting your finger off the one before. Can you hear how this joins the three notes together?

A new note

The tune below has a new note, called D, for your right hand. Here you can see where to find D on your piano, and how it is written on the staff.

In the treble clef, D sits just below the bottom line.

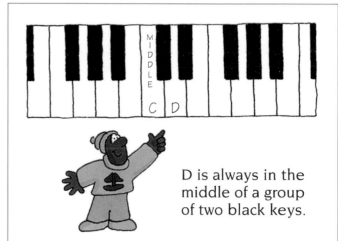

D is always in the middle of a group of two black keys.

Tune with D

In this tune, play middle C with your right thumb...

...and D with your first finger.

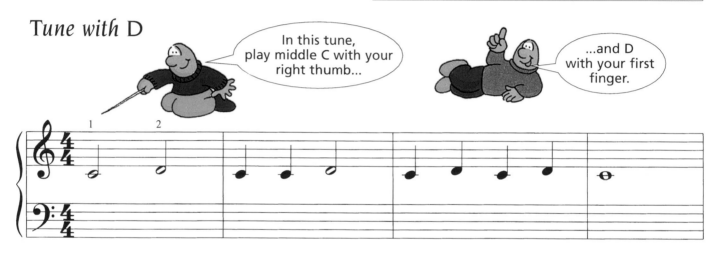

Piano fact

Grand pianos are bigger than other pianos. The strings inside are stretched out flat. Grand pianos can make a louder sound than ordinary pianos.

Grand pianos are usually used for concerts.

Another new note

On the right, you can see where to find the note B on your piano, and how it is written on the staff.

In the bass clef, B sits above the top line of the staff.

B is always to the right of a group of three black keys.

Play middle C, then B. Can you tell which one sounds lower?

A *tune with* B

The number two tells you to play B with your first finger.

Try to count in your head as you play.

Playing tip

The letter name of a note tells you which key to press on your piano.

This note is B.

Can you find every B on your piano?

Remember, the shape of a note tells you how many beats to count.

This note gets one beat.

Now the same note gets two beats.

Dotted notes

A dot after a note makes the note half as long again. A dotted minim lasts for three crotchet beats.

A new time signature

In three-four time, there are three crotchet beats in each bar.

Rocking song

This tune is in three-four time. Count to three before you start.

More notes and rhythms

The tune below has the note E in it. E is higher up on the staff than D, so it sounds higher.

This is what E looks like on the staff.

In the treble clef, E is on the bottom line of the staff.

E is always to the right of a group of two black keys.

Desert drums

Before you play this tune, try to name all of the notes. Then clap the rhythm.

Play E with your middle finger.

Another time signature

The tune below has a different time signature from the tunes you have played so far. It has two beats in each bar.

Clapping a rhythm

Here is a rhythm for you to clap in two-four time. It will help to count two beats before you begin.

Elephant march

Leaving gaps in music

Sometimes there are gaps in music when no sound is made. These gaps are called rests. There are symbols to tell you how long each rest lasts.

Rests

Each rest is named after the note shape with the same number of beats.

> Imagine this as a weak rest, which has to sit on the line. It only lasts for two beats.

 This is a semibreve rest. It lasts for four beats.

This is a minim rest. It lasts for two beats.

 This is a crotchet rest. It lasts for one beat.

> Imagine this as a strong rest which can hang off the line for four beats.

> When you see a rest, lift your finger off the piano...

> ...and count the number of beats in your head.

Clapping a rhythm

Clap and count this rhythm. When you see a rest, don't clap, but keep counting steadily.

> Don't clap here...

> ...but remember to keep counting.

A *tune with rests*

A new note

The tune below has a new note, called A, for your left hand.

In a group of three black keys, A is between the top two black keys.

Swan song

Tunes to play

Here are some tunes for you to play. Remember to look at the time signature at the beginning of each one, and count very carefully.

Note reminder

These are all the notes you have learned so far. Play them, and say the name of each note as you play.

Mary had a little lamb

Skating song

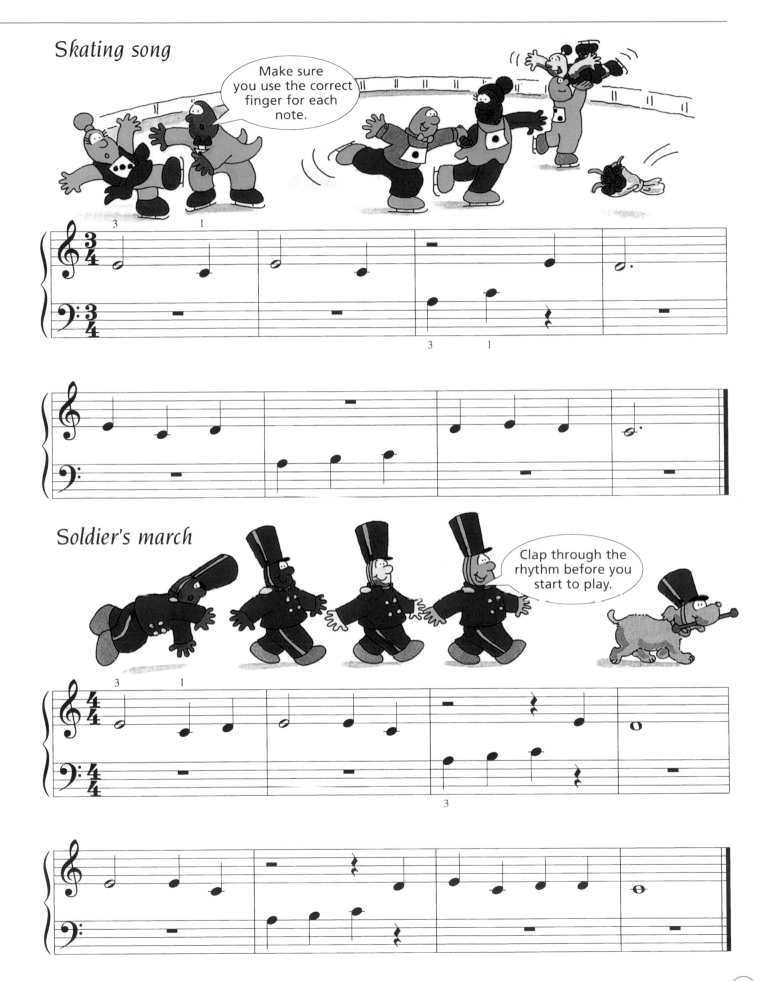

Soldier's march

New notes

The tune below uses two new notes, called F and G. Here you can learn to play F with your right hand and G with your left hand.

Playing G

Here you can find out about the note G.

In the bass clef, G sits in the space below the top line of the staff.

Playing F

Here you can find out about the note F.

In the treble clef, F sits in the space above the bottom line of the staff.

In a group of three black keys, G is to the right of the first black key.

F is always the white key to the left of a group of three black keys.

Yankee doodle

Tied notes

Sometimes two or more notes on the same line or space are joined together with a curved line.

These are called tied notes. The new note lasts for the same number of beats as both notes added together.

Count the beats

Here are four sets of tied notes. See if you can work out how many beats each set lasts for. The first one has been worked out for you already.

Lullaby

Both hands together

For the tunes on these two pages, you sometimes need to play with both hands at the same time.

Playing tip

When you first play a tune, try to keep going to the end. If you find some parts more difficult than others, practise these parts on their own a few times before you play the whole piece again.

Four o'clock

Shorter notes

On these two pages you can find out about a shorter note, called a quaver. A quaver lasts for half a crotchet beat.

New notes

On page 24, you learned how to play the note G with your left hand. Now you can learn to play G with your right hand.

You have already learned to play F with your right hand (see page 24). Here you can learn to play F with your left hand.

F is the white key to the left of a group of three black keys.

G is between the bottom two of a group of three black keys.

Clapping rhythms

When you play two quavers next to each other, it helps to say the word "and" for the second one. Try counting and clapping these rhythms.

Musette

Dotted crotchets

Remember, a dot after a note makes the note half as long again. So a dotted crotchet lasts for one and a half beats.

A rhythm with dotted crotchets

Try clapping the rhythm on the right. The dotted crotchet in the first bar is followed by a quaver. Clap the quaver on the "and" of the second beat of the bar.

Slow song

Find the sharps

Can you name these sharp notes? Try finding and playing them on your piano.

Find out the answers on page 63.

The bell ringers

In this tune, play F sharp with the middle finger of your right hand.

Practise going from G to F sharp a few times before you begin.

Remember to count five beats for the tied note.

Piano fact

The biggest grand piano ever made weighed 1.25 tonnes and was 3.55 metres long. It was made in London in 1935.

More about black keys

On page 32, you learned about sharp notes. Here you can learn about notes called flats.

Flats

A flat sign tells you to play the nearest black key just to the left of that note, with no keys in between. A flat sign in front of a note makes that note sound slightly lower.

This is a flat sign.

Like sharps, flat signs are written before the note.

This is B flat for your left hand.

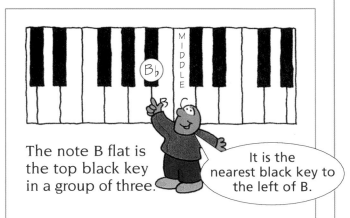

The note B flat is the top black key in a group of three.

It is the nearest black key to the left of B.

How flats work

Like sharp notes, when a note becomes flat, all the other notes in the same bar, on the same line or space, will also become flat. The effect of a flat sign only lasts for one bar.

These notes are both B flat.

This note is not B flat because it is in a new bar.

Swinging song

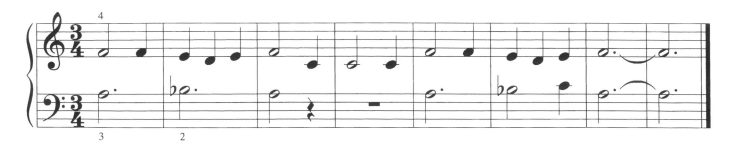

New notes

Here are three new notes for your right hand, called A, B and C.

B flat for your right hand

The tune below uses B flat for your right hand. See if you can find this B flat on your piano.

Country dance

Natural notes

Any note that isn't a sharp or a flat is called a natural note. Sometimes a special sign is used to show that a note is natural. Usually this is to cancel the effect of a sharp or flat sign earlier in the bar.

This is a natural sign.

This note is F sharp.

This note is F, or F natural.

The flat sign makes this note B flat.

This note is an ordinary B because of the natural sign.

Accidentals

A sharp, flat or natural sign written before a note is called an accidental. Here are the accidentals you have learned.

For a sharp, you play the nearest black key above.

For a flat, you play the nearest black key below.

A natural changes the sharp or flat into a white note.

A *tune with accidentals*

If you practise this tune often...

...it will help the fingers of your right hand to become stronger.

Ragtime capers

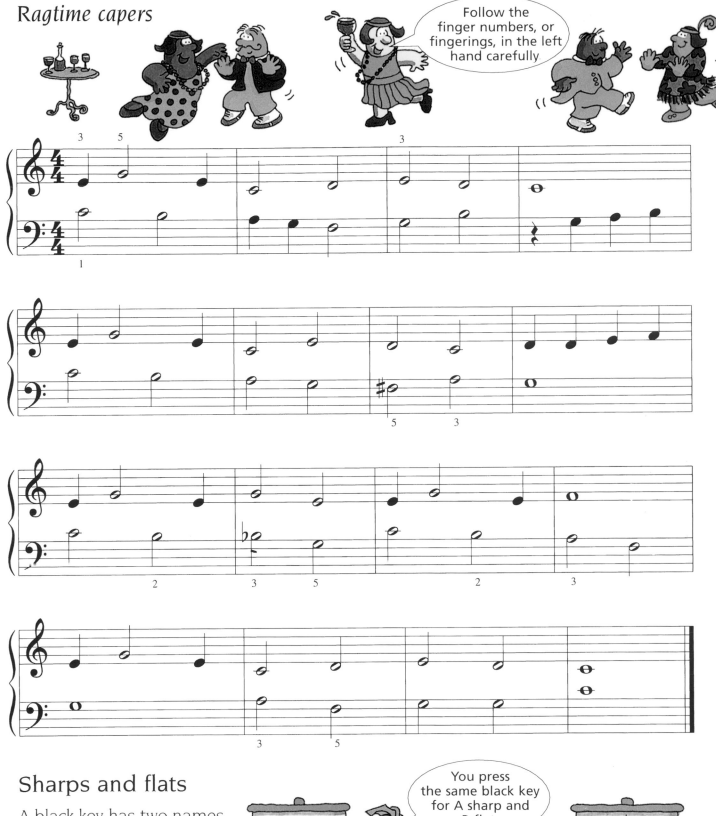

Follow the finger numbers, or fingerings, in the left hand carefully.

Sharps and flats

A black key has two names. It can be called a sharp after the white note to the left of it. It can also be called a flat after the white note to the right of it.

You press the same black key for A sharp and B flat.

A sharp

B flat

Scales and keys

A scale is a set of eight notes played one after the other. Scales begin and end on notes with the same name. There are several different types of scale. The most common type is called a major scale.

A major scale with white notes

The notes below make up the scale of C major for your right hand. This scale is made up only of white keys. Try playing it, following the fingerings very carefully.

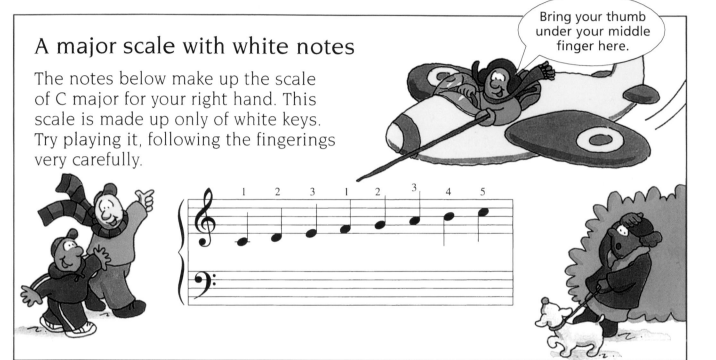

A scale with one flat

You can start a scale on any note on your piano. The scale of F major starts on the note F. Before you play it, can you find and name the last three notes?

Key signatures

The scale of F major has one flat, B flat. The flat sign is usually written after the treble clef, instead of in front of each B. When a sharp or flat sign is written here, it is called the key signature.

A tune which uses the notes in the scale of F major is said to be in the key of F major. The key signature is B flat. This tells you to play B flat instead of B all the way through the tune.

Pipers' march

Distances between notes

The distance between two notes is called an interval. There are lots of different types of interval. Here you can learn about some of them.

The distance from one key to the next key, above or below it, with no keys in between, is a semitone.

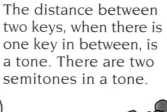

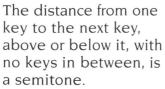
A semitone is the smallest interval.

The distance from F sharp to G is a semitone.

The distance between two keys, when there is one key in between, is a tone. There are two semitones in a tone.

The interval between D and E is a tone.

Interval quiz

Can you tell which of these intervals are semitones, and which are tones?

You can check your answers on page 63.

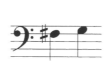

Octaves

The distance from one note to the next note above or below it, with the same letter name, is called an octave.

The interval between this C...

...and this C is called an octave.

More about scales and keys

Here you can see the notes that make up the scale of G major.

The scale of G can be written with the sharp at the beginning of the staff. So its key signature is F sharp.

Hippo waltz

This tune uses the notes in the scale of G major, so it is in the key of G. It has a key signature of one sharp. This key signature tells you to play F sharp instead of F throughout the tune.

Playing loudly and quietly

In music, there are special words that tell you how loudly or quietly to play. These words are usually in Italian, because music was first printed in Italy.

Quiet words

Here are some words that tell you how quietly to play.

To play quietly, press the keys lightly, but keep your fingers firm so that the notes sound properly.

Piano (pee-yah-no) means "quiet".

Mezzo (met-zo) *piano* means "fairly quiet".

Pianissimo (pee-yan-iss-ih-mo) means "very quiet".

Loud words

When you play loudly, don't thump the keys, but press them down firmly.

Forte (for-tay) means "loud".

Mezzo forte means "fairly loud".

Fortissimo means "very loud".

Instructions in music

The words for loud and quiet are often shortened to one or two letters. These letters are written between the staves.

Try playing the exercise below, making each note just a little louder than the one before.

Rain dance

Remember, the key signature used in this tune means that you play all the Bs as B flats.

Repeats in music

At the end of some tunes, there is a sign called a repeat mark. This tells you to go back to the beginning and play the music again.

This is a repeat mark.

Repeating part of a tune

Sometimes just part of a tune needs to be repeated. In this case, repeat marks are written before and after the part you have to repeat.

When you first see this sign, ignore it and play on.

At this sign, go back to the first sign and repeat the section.

When you reach the second sign again, ignore it and play to the end.

If you number the bars in this example from 1 to 6, this the order you would play them in.

1 2 3 4 3 4 5 6

Repeating from the beginning

In some tunes, you repeat part of the music from the beginning. When this happens, there is only one repeat mark. This is the one with the dots on the left.

When you reach this sign, go back and play the music from the start.

Ignore this sign the second time you reach it.

New notes

The tune below uses three new notes for your left hand, called C, D and E.

How fast to play

The speed of a tune is called its *tempo*. Some tunes have an Italian word at the beginning to tell you how fast or slow you should play. Here you can find out what some of the words mean.

Allegro (a-leg-ro) means "fast".

A lively dance tune might be played *allegro*.

Lento (len-to) is the Italian word for "slow".

A sad song might be played *lento*.

Andante (an-dan-tay) is a speed in between *largo* and *allegro*. It means "at a walking pace".

Playing tip

Before you play a tune, it helps to look through the music very carefully. Here are some of the things to look out for.

How many beats are there in each bar?

What is the key signature of the tune?

What do all the signs and words mean?

March

Andante

Very short notes

Sometimes in music there are very short notes called semiquavers. A semiquaver looks like a quaver with an extra tail. It lasts for half a quaver beat.

Semiquavers and quavers can be joined like this.

This is a semiquaver.

Two or more semiquavers are often joined together, like this.

Two semiquavers are the same length as one quaver.

This is a semiquaver rest.

It means that you leave a gap of one semiquaver beat.

Clapping a rhythm

Here is a rhythm for you to clap. The counts written under the notes will help you.

Balloon ride

Try not to rush the quavers and semiquavers.

Just keep counting steadily.

Andante

D.C. al Fine

D.C. *al Fine* stands for *Da Capo al Fine*. This tells you to go back to the beginning of the piece and play the music again, until you reach the word *Fine* (fee-nay). Then stop playing.

Traffic jam

First and second endings

Sometimes a repeated section has two different endings. The first time through, play the bar marked "1". The second time, skip this, and play the bar marked "2".

If you number the bars in this example from 1 to 5, this is the order you would play them in.

Come to the fair

Allegro

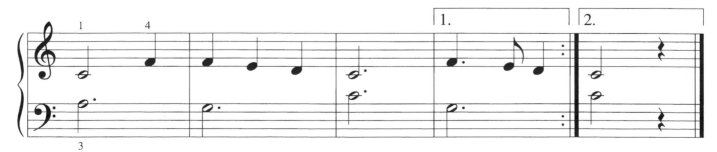

Getting louder and quieter

There are Italian words and symbols that tell you to get gradually louder or quieter. The Italian word for "get louder" is *crescendo* (cresh-en-doe). The Italian word for "get quieter" is *diminuendo* (dim-in-you-en-doe).

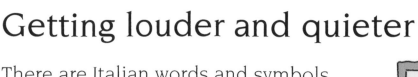

The first symbol below tells you to get gradually louder.

This symbol tells you to get gradually quieter.

These words are often shortened to *cresc.* and *dim.*

mp

cresc.

dim.

In piano music, the words and symbols are written between the staves.

Start to get louder at the beginning of the symbol...

...and keep getting louder until you reach the end of the symbol.

Remembering the symbols

To help you remember what each symbol means, think of what it looks like.

The symbol for *crescendo* starts small. It gets bigger as you get louder.

The symbol for *diminuendo* starts big, but gets smaller as you get quieter.

An example to try

You can practise getting louder and quieter by playing this tune a few times. Get gradually louder in the first bar, and quieter near the end of the second bar.

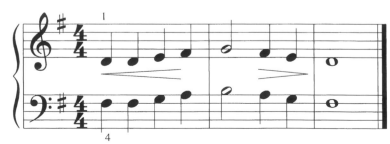

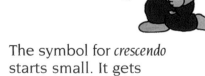

A new time signature

In six-eight time, the six tells you that there are six beats in each bar. The eight tells you they are quaver beats.

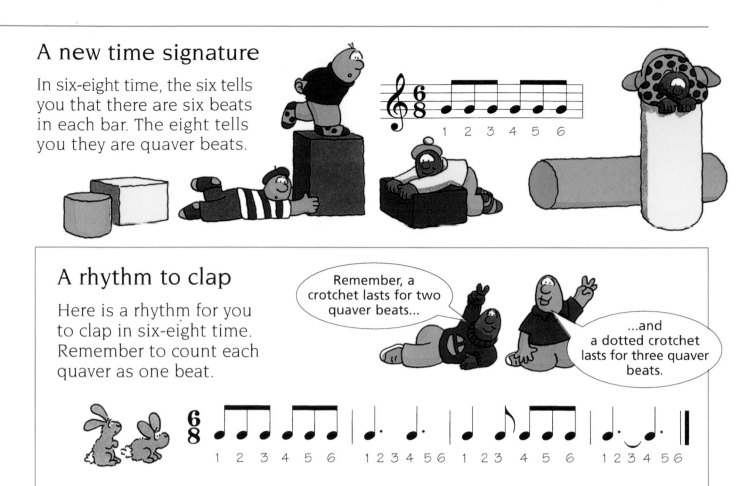

A rhythm to clap

Here is a rhythm for you to clap in six-eight time. Remember to count each quaver as one beat.

Remember, a crotchet lasts for two quaver beats...

...and a dotted crotchet lasts for three quaver beats.

Daniel's jig

To play the F sharp in the last bar...

...you need to cross your first finger over your thumb.

Playing smoothly and jerkily

Until now, you have played notes smoothly, with no breaks in between. This is called playing *legato* (leg-ah-toe).

The word *legato* is often written between the staves.

Playing *staccato*

The opposite of *legato* is *staccato* (stack-ah-toe). Notes played *staccato* are not joined together. This makes the music sound jerky.

To play *staccato*, you need to strike the key very quickly and sharply. Take your finger off as soon as you have pressed the key.

Staccato notes have a dot above or below them.

To play *staccato*, your fingers need to be very firm.

Try not to play *staccato* notes louder than the others.

Staccato stomp

Allegro

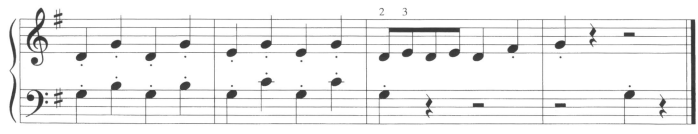

Jellytown blues

Musical sentences

When you talk to someone, the words are grouped together in sentences. In the same way, music has sentences, called phrases.

Phrases

A phrase is a section of a tune. It is usually made up of a number of bars, and can sound like a short tune in itself.

At the end of a phrase, lift your hand a little to make a slight break before you begin the next phrase. Imagine you are a singer taking a breath.

Questions and answers

When you make sentences, you can use questions and answers. Musical phrases can also be like questions and answers. The first phrase below is like a question.

The tune does not sound complete unless you add the second phrase. This is like an answer. When you play both phrases, the tune sounds complete.

Incy, wincy spider

Tunes to play

The tunes on these two pages are all Christmas carols.

We three kings of Orient are

Remember to look at the key signatures before you start to play.

Jingle bells

Allegro

Good King Wenceslas

Tunes for two people

Tunes for two people are called duets. The tune below is for two people to play at the same time on one piano. Both players need to sit side by side. You could play with your teacher or a friend.

If you are sitting on the left-hand side of the piano, play the music on this page (Part B). If you are sitting on the right-hand side, play the music on the opposite page (Part A).

Air (Part B)

Air (Part A)

More tunes to play

Here are some more tunes for you
to play. Remember to look through
the music before you start.

Russian round

From 'The new world'

Music words

The list here explains most of the
music words used in this book.

Allegro	Play the music fast.	**Key signature**	Sharps or flats at the beginning of the staff.
Andante	Play the music at a walking pace.	**Ledger line**	Extra lines for notes that are too high or low to fit on the staff.
Crescendo	Get gradually louder.		
Da Capo al Fine	Go back to the beginning and repeat the music until you reach the word *Fine*.	*Legato*	Play very smoothly.
		Lento	Play the music slowly.
		Mezzo forte	Play fairly loudly.
Diminuendo	Get gradually quieter.	*Mezzo piano*	Play fairly quietly.
Dotted note	A dot after a note makes the note half as long again.	**Octave**	The distance between two notes with the same letter name. There are eight notes in an octave.
Duet	A piece of music for two players.		
Fine	The end of the music (see *Da Capo al Fine*).	*Pianissimo*	Play very quietly.
		Piano	Play the music quietly.
Forte	Play the music loudly.	**Scale**	A set of eight notes that begins and ends on notes with the same letter name.
Fortissimo	Play the music very loudly.		
Interval	The distance between two notes.		
Key	The letter name of the scale on which the music is based.	**Semitone**	The smallest interval between two notes, for example, F to F sharp.

Staccato	A dot above or below a note. *Staccato* notes should be very short and spiky.	**Time signature**	Numbers at the start of the music that tell you how many beats are in each bar, and what kind of beats they are.
Tie	A curved line joining two notes on the same line or space. Add the lengths of the notes together.	**Tone**	An interval of two semitones, for example, between F and G.

Answers

Page 25

4 + 2 = 6   1 + 1 = 2   1 + 2 = 3   2 + 2 = 4

Page 33

D sharp   G sharp   G sharp   C sharp

Page 38

The top three notes in the scale of F major are D, E, and F.

Page 40

Semitone   Semitone   Tone   Tone

Tone   Semitone

Page 41

The top four notes in the scale of G major are D, E, F sharp and G.

Index

Notes

This edition first published in 2003 by Usborne Publishing, Usborne House, 83-85 Saffron Hill, London EC1N 8RT, England. Copyright © 2003, 1998, 1991, 1988 Usborne Publishing Ltd. First published in America in March 1995. The name Usborne and the devices ♀ ⊕ are Trade Marks of Usborne Publishing Ltd. All rights reserved. No part of this publication may be reproduced, stored in a retrieval system or transmitted in any form or by any means electronic, mechanical, photocopying, recording or otherwise, without prior permission of the publisher. Printed in China.